My First 100 Unbelievable Days

Buffalo Arts Publishing

My First 100 Unbelievable Days. Copyright © 2017 by Donald T. Scheller. Printed in the United States of America. All rights reserved. No part of this book may be reproduced or transmitted in any form or by any means without written permission of the author. For information, address Buffalo Arts Publishing, 179 Greenfield Drive, Tonawanda, NY 14150

Email: info@buffaloartspublishing.com

Cover image from a painting by Edward G. Bisone, 2000, used by permission from the estate of E. G. Bisone

ISBN 978-0-9978741-2-9

My First 100 Unbelievable Days

January 20, 2017

Today begins the new
age. A.T. or After Trump.
How long can it last?

They're having a ball.
I'm having my own bawl,
crying for the world.

Who decides what is
"fake news"? Truth? Will there ever
be more elections?

One can hope Trump will
be what unifies both parties
to impeach him.

January 23

They didn't want more
politics as usual
so they chose chaos.

Trump's idea of
draining the swamp was to
make it his cabinet.

Politics, like art;
it's what they say it is and
not what it looks like.

If you didn't vote
you got what you deserved
and prayer won't help.

Do they really believe
what they say or is it to
hold onto their jobs?

His voters, like himself,
believing the last thing
they hear. (so sad)

Even a bad craftsman
couldn't build a cabinet
as bad as Trump has.

If three times they say,
answer the question, come up
with alternate facts.

January 24

Pharoah Trump's first acts;
destroy his predecessor's
chance for legacy.

Which first, popular vote and
crowd size concern or non-ego
related matters?

Make America
great again? Which spelling
of great (grate) did he mean?

January 25

We know Trump won.
We just don't know who the real
president is.

Supreme commander
of the world is better than
being president.

Who needs truth when
alternative facts replace
obvious falsehoods?

Make America
great again is wrong. It's make
Trump even greater!

Can alternative
facts only exist in an
alternative universe?

Four bankruptcies yet
they elect him and give him
budgets to create.

January 26

First thing we do is
destroy Obama's legacy,
then the world.

We've entered a new
phase with Trump; government
by intuition.

The Bully Pulpit
resurrected. Why aren't
they calling it that?

The Affordable
Care Act will now be replaced
with prayer. Start praying.

Government by
tweet, twitter, bullying and
alternative fact.

January 27

The Cult of Trump;
all thinking suspended, all
tweets oracular.

We wanted a president;
we got last thought best thought,
until retweeted.

He says...; then his minions
said what he really said meant
something different.

Trump's reality,
presented, then re-presented,
representing what?

What will it take for
his voters to realize
they voted wrong?

Is your president
setting the wrong precedent?
Are you still happy?

January 28

If Trump had common
sense, would he be more or
less dangerous?

For Trump, there seems no
line or distinction between
a lie or the truth.

When will his people
realize their president
is damaged goods?

Trump's attention span
is one hundred and forty
characters, or less.

With Trump president,
Republicans finally
will learn tolerance.

Will the real Trump be
as entertaining as
SNL's faux Trump?

The sad thing is that
many believe Trump must be
more than he seems to be.

Trump's cabinet
is his slap in the face
to America.

The most honest part
of Trump's personality
is his ego.

January 31

Tomorrow now seems
less guaranteed than any
time in my past.

The extravagance
of vacuous thought defines
Trump's presidency.

Suddenly, with last
nights firing and hiring,
Trump becomes Nixon. (A.G. let go.)

Trumpolini or
Trumpler or Hitrump or
Trumao or what?

Lies so easily
slip from their lips as though they
didn't fear affect.

I thought Trump as
president could only
happen as fiction.

February 2

Tragicomedy's
history begins anew
with Trump's presidency.

How soon before if
we disagree with Trump we're
enemies of the state?

Is it president
Trump or president Bannon?
Was he on the ballot?

February 3

Is it the right person for
the position or a major
contributor reward?

It's not enough to
have facts on your side when they
have alternative facts.

February 4

Being elected
president doesn't really
mean he's president.

February 7

The swamp, as promised,
has been drained. Trump has hired or
appointed them all.

If the "so called judge"
is proper, then so is the
so called president.

Unless Trump says it,
the rest being reported
is just fake news.

Playing bridge with Trump:
spades are never trump, nor women,
Muslims, Mexicans, truth...

President for life?
The constitution doesn't
matter to him.

What once mattered
no longer does as long as
we're in power now.

The ego of him;
holding up all he signs like
a kid with a new drawing.

Polarity:
north and south poles, democrats
and republicans.

The ego of him;
the landslide wasn't and the
election was rigged.

Government of the
party by the party for
the party. We don't count.

If he needs to be
best at everything, would being
the best worst count?

Has Trump forgotten
there are immigrants in
his family tree?

February 8

Two many egos
in one White House. Bannon
has to go. So sad.

Will there be a phoenix
left to rise from the ashes
of democracy?

The whole world is
watching! Resurrect the chant.
It's needed again.

Might ain't always right.
It's often destructive
in the wrong hands.

Power, in the wrong
hands, is like a child with
a loaded pistol.

Trump learned from watching
Costanza on Seinfeld: it's not
a lie if you believe it.

The doomsday clock
ticks a bit faster of late
as we near its midnight.

Have we learned nothing
from Mussolini, Hitler,
Stalin and their like?

February 9

Off the cuff remarks
show Trump's true intellect – none,
just assigning blame.

Think like Trump. No, wait.
Act like Trump. There's no thinking
necessary.

Most of us have
an I.Q. Trump, instead, only
has I,I,I,I.

The only wall Trump
has built so far is around
himself, and it's crumbling.

Worked for Hitler
doesn't mean it'll work for Trump.
I hope we've learned something.

It's no surprise Trump's
rounded mouth looks like an anal
sphincter. Look what comes out.

First badmouth the press,
then denigrate judges, then
be judge and jury.

To err is human
but to tweet and err daily
is Trump's domain.

It's politics as
unusual with Trump and
not as usual.

Trump should be labeled
as a risk to our health first
and welfare second.

February 10

Mortification:
what we who didn't vote for
Trump are now feeling.

Does what he tweeted
become what he really meant?
What do you believe?

It's hard to know what
someone who doesn't think
is really thinking.

When Trump falls, will it be
the domino theory or
as the house of cards?

February 13

Sometimes you win not
because you're you but because
you're not the other.

Trump's first hundred days
results in my first worst
one hundred daze.

The horror of the
imponderable now
ponderable. How?

February 14

Intellect or guile;
which best serves a president?
Trump has ego and lies.

Trump never loses
even if he doesn't win.
Ego won't allow it.

Trump, posing with his
executive orders as if
he read or wrote them.

When will they muster
the courage to stand up to
Trump and do the right thing?

The Capone of Trump,
getting appointed henchmen
to do his dirty work.

Have we forgotten
what democracy is? It's
not autocracy.

In like Flynn, out like Flynn.
He didn't lie, he forgot.
He resigned? He was fired?

February 15

News fascinates me,
wondering who's next to go
who won't worship Trump.

The lesson of Flynn:
blind obedience to Trump
doesn't always help.

Republican spin:
how dare the CIA
monitor citizens!

The daily self-destructing
of a party, of our
democracy.

Republican spin:
it's all the fault of those not in
power, those Democrats.

How much of Spicer
can he prostitute before
there's no Spicer left?

The new Nixon years;
Watergate revisited
in case you missed it.

I'm thankful for leaks
plumbers haven't been able
to find the source of.

How many people
are now sorry they didn't vote?
Have they learned from this?

February 16

New day
new controversy
as usual

Of repeal appeal:
it works in elections but
not as policy.

Leaks are good if it
hurts my foes. Leaks are bad
when they affect Trump.

Will Trump replace the
intelligence agencies
with intuitive ones?

Trump seems determined
to dismantle national
security. Why?

I still say, if I
didn't vote for him, then he's
not my president.

He's more contentious
than he is conscientious,
ruling by instinct.

Each day, more fake news
if not from his mouth or his
appointed minions.

I think Trump wanted
to be elected president
but not to be one.

When will they realize
he's not fit to be president
and impeach him?

Trump has hired those
to join his club whose clubs
he couldn't join.

February 17

Did Trump hire the swamp
he said he'd drain just to
keep an eye on them?

Trump is never wrong.
He's just been given the wrong
facts by his people.

Even Morning Joe
has begun to turn on Trump.
Will his base turn on him?

Trump's outlook on race:
There are winners and losers
in any race. Yes?

Trump wins, Putin wins.
The losers? America
and democracy.

The only legacy
I'm concerned about is our
country's after Trump.

Trump's first hundred days
are as compelling to watch
as Nixon's last days.

February 18

Seeing and hearing Trump
is like Saturday Night Live
every day. So sad.

Shock humor: just when
I thought it was outdated
Trump gets elected.

Trump's so bad he spells
ego with an I, and it's
always capitalized.

Trump hates free speech
because there's no money to
be made from something free.

Playing to the crowd
is fine if you're a comic
but Trump's just a joke.

Can I respect the
office of the president
but not the president?

Most springs have a
better memory than Trump
and they don't lie.

Trump makes George Dubya
look like a great president
and almost Nixon, too.

February 21

Which is more correct;
who's president or
whose president?

First Trump says or tweets it,
then his people rush to say
what he really meant.

What about Sweden?
Can you believe it? Sweden!
No one believed it.

Is everyone who
voted for Trump as president
still glad they did?

What will replace
democracy as we know it?
Autocracy? Trumpocracy?

If you voted for Trump
it must be a private joke
because I don't get it.

Is presidential
fallout worse than nuclear
fallout? Are there shelters?

Trump speaks a language
only Spicer and Conway
seem able to decipher.

February 22

Each day, a new
outrage depending on your
affiliation.

If Trump is really
a dictator in training,
who are his mentors?

The courts are our
enemy. The press is also
our enemy.

I will not
not be noticed. I am
your president!

Stand on principle
or work together to
accomplish something?

If Trump's first thirty
days seem like a year, what will
four years seem like?

They've had seven years
to fix Obamacare;   how will
they do it in months?

When they say patience,
which spelling are they using?
Wait? Or those in need?

Executive Orders:
his only contribution
is his signature.

Trump's dictum, borrowed
loosely from the Lord's Prayer;
my will be done!

Trump's presidency
is in its infancy, and
led by a child.

February 23

It's pretty bad when
our president must rely
on interpreters.

If going overseas,
remember to wear your Not
My President button.

Imagine Trump's
dismay when he discovered
his word wasn't the law.

February 24

Welcome to the new
rising United States of Trump,
built on promises.

Freedom of the press:
Trump decides who is granted
that needed freedom.

How much spinning does
it take before the truth is
no longer the truth?

February 27

Surely one man can't
destroy democracy, can he?
Again?

Yes, Trump needs the press.
His vanity requires
constant attention.

Deport Muslims and
Mexicans. Who's next? Catholics?
Baptists? Democrats?

I know people who stopped
doing the Times crossword puzzles because
the Times is too Liberal.

You wanted Trump.
You got him. Live with it.
Pretend all is well.

With Trump, what you see
is all you're ever going
to get. Live with that.

I used to read
fantasy. Now I just watch
the news all day.

February 28

If Trump doesn't respect
the office of the president,
why should I respect him?

Outrage on outrage.
Hillary leaks were good.
Trump leaks are treason.

I call Trump Big Bird
for all his constant tweeting
with nothing said.

Trump says what his base
wants to hear and even he
starts to believe it.

March 1

Special interests
always wins out over those
with less or no money.

Is it still fake news if
they have film of him saying
what he said he didn't?

How can those closest
to Trump remain silent
knowing how he lies?

Almost anyone can
act presidential for
a speech or a day.

The truth, for Trump, is
often directly opposite
of what he says it is.

March 2

Consciously not
writing about Trump is
writing about Trump.

How distorted facts
before they become old lies
presented as news.

The only wall Trump
builds is the one surrounding
his presidency.

Is all truth hidden
beneath peeling layers of lies
or just in politics?

For Trump there is
no transubstantiation.
He is what he is.

I'm more afraid of
Trump's presidency than
I am of dying.

March 3

The buck always seems
to stop one person before
Trump. He didn't know!

Some look like puppets,
others act like puppets, all
doing Trump's bidding.

It's never Trump's fault.
It's Obama's, Hillary's,
Democrats, the press.

Sessions didn't lie,
he just presented the facts
incorrectly. Huh?

Trump would never sell
our democracy away
just for money ... would he?

March 4

Does Trump, like popes old,
award indulgences to
the highest bidders?

Is it possible
too much Mar-a-Largo has
given Trump sunstroke?

Is not understanding
Trump's other meanings of the
use of words our fault?

What experience
is needed to become a
Trump spin doctor?

March 6

With Trump, no news is
good news, unless it persists.
Then I'm suspicious.

Who's left to insult?
Putin? Catholics? God? Take
Trump's tweeting away!

Facts needn't really
exist. They just have to
exist in Trump's mind.

Home of the whopper;
not Burger King, the White House
with Trump's mad tweeting.

Fantasy Island,
otherwise known as where Trump
resides and tweets.

They can't say Trump lies
but it's okay to say he's too
often untruthful.

March 7

Could Saturday's tweet
about Obama's "taping" be the
tweet to end all tweets?

What Ben Carson taught me:
the slaves brought on slave ships were
really immigrants.

Jabberwocky:
tweets chasing white rabbits
only Trump can see.

Listening to Trump
often brings to mind Lewis Carroll's
Alice in Wonderland.

Those who refuse to
be Trump's cabinet picks are
who I respect most.

The White House functions
as theater of the absurd.
Hold applause to the end.

March 8

Obama didn't
call it Obamacare. The
Republicans did.

Is it the first one
hundred days or the first or worst
hundred daze of Trump?

March 9

You can't excuse what
he says saying that's just Trump.
He's the president!

Can he declare the
country bankrupt as he has
his business ventures?

Has Trump forgotten
his present wife was also
an immigrant?

In Trump's mind, an
unproven fact is as real as
one that can be proved.

I fear the act it
will take for Trump's base to see
how wrong they were.

I didn't lose sleep
Election Day but I have
been ever since.

March 11

Job numbers were fake
news before. Now they're good, they're real
says Spicer, grinning.

The fictions of Trump;
would his tax returns turn them
to reality?

I've lost faith in all
the voters who've forgotten the
politicians work for us.

Thank you for electing
me president. Promises made
may not be kept.

Trump fires all who do
not worship, bow down to him or
remain subservient.

March 12

It's not personal
style; it's his not acting
presidential.

More frightening than
Trump is his base that believes
he's doing a good job.

Trump's great achievement:
making Reagan, Nixon and
Bush look good to great.

March 13

Do we take Trump
literally, seriously
or symbolically?

His rallies are
really ego boosts. He's
addicted to applause.

He said "wiretapped".
They said he meant all aspects
of surveillance.

Another rally?
Doesn't he realize the
election is over.

For Trump: prove it or
retract it. We know he won't
apologize.

It's the party first,
before truth, honor, conscience
and us, your employers.

Is Spicer really
convinced his lies are truth?
How long does that take?

Spicer and Conway;
how do you live with yourself?
Do you know what truth is?

March 14

Tweet insurance? To
protect corporations and
people from Trump's tweets?

Bannon intimates,
Trump follows, thinking it's
his original thought.

If Trump and Bannon
see China as the enemy,
then what is Russia?

Millions may lose their
health coverage but it will
cost the government less.

The primary reason
not to support a bad bill;
not being re-elected.

March 15

There's news, Fox News, fake
news, what Trump says and what
Spicer said he meant.

March 17

So he didn't
wiretap me. I still
won't apologize.

All this spinning,
Don't Trump, Spicer and Conway
ever get dizzy?

Okay, it wasn't
Obama. Then it must be
British Intelligence.

Trump or Bannon?
Who did they really elect
as president?

March 18

Trump crosses yet
another country he's
insulted off his list.

Trump meets with Merkel,
makes lame joke, talks about himself
and ignores her.

The politicians,
this president, do they not
have families, loved ones?

March 19

Trump won't apologize
but maybe he'll walk it back
a little, maybe.

March 20

You can tell a lot
about someone by their handshake,
or how they won't.

Trump may never be
known for his sincerity
or his intellect.

Can America
file for Chapter 11
bankruptcy under Trump?

Germany, Britain,
Australia, Mexico, China:
who's next on Trump's list?

March 21

Commander in cheat?
Commander in tweet?
But never the chief.

Why does Trump refer
to himself in the third person?
How many are there?

Has Trump confused
freedom of the press with
freedom from the press?

Is it Trump needs
publicity or Trump's
publicity needs?

The presidency
as a commodity; could
it happen? Has it?

"1984"
suddenly in demand in bookstores
since Trump's presidency.

Nobody ever
said what they said after it's
spun and restated.

March 22

Did Trump want to be
president to leave office
as rich as he's claimed he is?

No ability
or credibility.
What else can he lose?

Don't delude yourself.
What you see is all there is.
There's no hidden depth.

March 23

Repeal it now!
I don't care about the cost.
I promised I would.

Everyone but Trump
says he lied about Obama
wiretapping him.

New lies surface to
change an ever changing
narrative of lies.

One term president?
How about just a hundred
day president?

How do you pressure
politicians to vote for
what they know is wrong?

They didn't know the
Affordable Care Act was
Obamacare! Did Trump?

"I guess I can't be doing
so badly because I'm president
and you're not". (Trump in TIME article)

March 24

Nope, there's only a
Plan A. When will Spicer
learn moderation?

Obamacare stays.
The art of the steal loses.
Trump Care dead for now.

Trump still pretends the
ACA is evil and soon
Democrats will beg for change.

Don't blame Democrats,
Trump. Your party had the votes
needed by themselves.

March 25

Tax reform next from
Trump who hasn't paid taxes
in how many years?

March 27

Is Trump beginning
to change? No malicious tweets
over the weekend.

Sometimes it's hard to
tell friends from enemies
in politics.

Our democracy
on the world stage: we're all
holding our breath.

Has Trump ever learned
from past mistakes? What do his
four bankruptcies tell you?

Why does the White House
try to hide Trump's golf trips?
Is he a bad golfer?

March 28

Nunes proves he's just
another Trump or Bannon flunky.
How do we dismiss him?

Trump priority:
corporate wealth comes before
the environment.

Trump reaches a new low
in two months that it took Obama
three years to reach (poll numbers).

It's not the president's
job to know everything but
he should know something.

Since global warming
is a hoax, Obama's
directives are gone.

Trump: What's bad for the
environment is good for
jobs; thus new order.

March 29

Mercurial
personalities have no
place in politics.

Russian Dressing
metaphors? Spicer now as
rude as Trump is.

Trump, what will you do
when there's no one left to blame?
Will they still trust you?

No civility
No credibility
No way to govern.

Trump's White House drama,
like a weekly TV show
but played out daily.

March 30

If the press is Trump's
enemy, why is he always
pandering to it?

Bad week for Trump.
Time for another rally
or photo op.

Is Trump really
the lesser of two evils?
What a way to vote.

Trump, Jared, Ivanka;
a presidency or
a monarchy?

March 31

One president and
many lap dogs fighting to
be the favorite.

The new space shuttle:
shuttling for position
in the new White House.

Flynn's innocent and
will testify but demands
immunity. Huh?

Trump's threat: Do what
I want or I'll make sure you're
not re-elected.

TIME says Trump's not a
liar, he's a fabulist.
Check your Thesaurus.

April 1

Is it a conflict
of interests or ethics,
the Trump businesses?

Trump planes, hotels, hats, golf
courses, clothing: the newest
branding of America.

With president Trump
it seems as if every day
is April Fools' Day.

Someone should tell Trump
it's not really true or proof
when it's in the Enquirer.

Has Trump forgotten
Obama is no longer
president but that he is?

April 2

Trump's repetition,
is it so he or we will
know what he's saying?

Has Trump ever done
anything wrong or Obama
anything right on Fox News?

Two Days of Infamy:
Pearl Harbor and Trump being
elected president.

April 3

The tweeting returns:
Trump's mental stability
questioned on TV.

Trump: first I watch Fox News,
then I read the Enquirer,
then I tweet at night.

Trump listens to no
advice from anyone but
trusts his gut instincts.

Trump still tweeting
about Hillary getting the
questions to be asked in debates.

Trump has never been
on my prayer list for his
continued good health.

Only Trump can use
unnamed sources but not
the enemy press.

Only Fox News stands
up to the fake liberal
news media. – Trump

Does anyone else
equate Fox News
with Pravda?

Is the lesser of
two evils Trump or Pence,
or even Ryan?

Am I as fixated
on Trump as Trump is on
Hillary and Obama?

None of the Trumps seem
qualified for the
positions they're in.

Can the United States
declare bankruptcy? It seems
to be Trump's style.

April 4

Of course the Supreme
Court is political. So
are vendettas.

No more party of
the people. Now it's party
for the corporations.

The people whisper,
big money shouts … drowning out
party and people.

The array of
politics might better
be called disarray.

Politics at work:
If we can't get what we want,
we'll change the rules. (Gorsuch nomination)

Let us hope that the
nuclear option remains
just in the senate.

If they can change rules,
can they also try to change
the Constitution?

With Trump in office
no news is good news or is it
no tweets are good news?

If Obama did it,
it's bad and will be changed
even if it's good.

Going backwards
while moving forward defines
politics today.

Easy politics:
If it's good, take credit for it; if
it's bad, they did it.

April 5

Chemical weapons used
in Syria. As usual, it's
Obama's fault.

Trump's poll numbers low;
who will he declare war on
to see them rise?

Putin finally
figured out to destroy
democracy – Trump!

New low poll numbers.
Time for another rally?
Maybe a parade?

Health care? The old pay
more, the young less; if you're poor
 and can't, say good-bye.

I could respect a
Republican president,
just not Donald Trump.

Trump picks another
victim without any proof.
Susan Rice. Who's next?

April 6

Trump bids good-bye to
Bannon at the big table.
Now he's president.

With Bannon gone
maybe we'll finally find
who's really in charge.

We know who is
president but we still
don't know who's in charge.

Trump, the elephant
in any room, whether he's
discussed or not.

Why Mar-a-Largo
to meet China's president?
Why not the White House?

Nunes steps aside.
Another manufactured
controversy gone.

April 7

Putin says Trump's strike
on Syria an act of aggression.
What was the Ukraine?

Trump as president;
an imitation of life
as we once knew it.

April 8

Obama needed
congressional approval
for Syria. Trump doesn't?

War in the White House,
Kushner versus Bannon. Does
it matter who wins?

April 10

What a surprise; mixed
messages from Trump White House
on Syria.

April 11

New book out on Trump's
charitable giving. He's
his own charity.

Was Syria bombing
only outrage or to boost
low poll numbers?

Will the next hundred
days, or three years, be any
different from these first ones?

Poor Spicer, always
having to restate, to say
what they really meant.

"...on message with the
president." How when he keeps
changing his mind?

Michael Cohen, Trump's
apologist; Trump knows what's
instinctively right.

Spicer's gaffe: Hitler's
gassing not as bad as Assad's.
What I meant was...

April 12

Spicer apologizes
for botched gassing statement,
something Trump can't do.

The saga continues,
more Trump appointees and staff
with Russian connections.

Same old act,
statement, restatement,
then denial.

Day 83, Trump
still referring to crooked
Hillary.

Bannon leaking
about Kushner leaking; I
wonder who'll remain.

Another date on
our timeline: B.C., A.D.,
A.T. – After Trump.

Spicer agrees with
Christie not to bring up
Hitler again.

Is Spicer's job safe?
With Trump's presidency, is
anyone's job safe?

Is Trump credible?
How many role reversals
before it isn't?

April 13

Credibility:
Do you have any if you
keep changing your views?

It's not the fact that
Hillary lost; it's that
Trump was the winner.

Are Republicans
now claiming Trump's changing views
are an asset?

Putin and Trump
represent two major powers
and two major egos.

Now, according to
Trump, Bannon is just a guy
who works for me.

Once Trump heard Bannon
was his brains, Bannon was
on his way out.

It's hard for me
to imagine Trump as
a strategist.

Some are more afraid
of Pence as president than
Trump as president.

April 14

MOAB! Hah!
My bomb is bigger than your bomb
and I have more.

I've done more in eight weeks
than Obama did in eight years!
We're ready for war.

Bombing as warning
or diversion from Russia ties?
Both bother me.

Is it how far from
war are we or how close
to a war are we?

Easter Egg Roll at
White House scaled back due to lack
of preparation. Sound familiar?

April 15

Transparency:
You can't see my tax returns or
White House visitor logs.

Which Trump line on China,
Russia, NATO or draining the
swamp do you believe?

Does Sessions see himself
as the new Goebels?
Is he proud of this?

April 17

The swamp has been drained.
All the pond scum is contained
in the White House now.

Trump tweets; put the
election behind you but
not him, just us.

If they can't plan an
Easter egg event, how can
they run a country?

China was the
enemy in March. Now in
April, they're allies.

Trump and Kim Jong-Un:
I dare you! Oh yeah, well
I double dare you!

April 18

Posturing is fine
but not with madmen with
nuclear weapons.

Saber rattling
is one thing but who fights with
sabers anymore?

Ideology
begins with I, the same I
manifesting ego.

How many Executive
Orders has Trump taken
credit for so far?

Why not show his tax
returns? What would they show?
It's guilt by omission.

Once you finally
realize a Trump promise
means nothing, what then?

Trump's hypocrisy:
Mar-a-Largo hires
foreign staff.

Trump's hypocrisy:
His son's vineyards hire
foreign workers.

Trump's hypocrisy:
His suits and Ivanka's clothing
line are made overseas.

April 19

I haven't heard of
or from Priebus in weeks.
Is he still around?

April 20

Tytrumpius Rex,
king of all world leaders,
at least in his mind.

Trump's armada
wasn't going where he thought.
Did anyone know?

April 21

Could Trump be priming
Ivanka or Kushner as our
next presidents?

Golf, bad for Obama,
good for Trump, as are his
Mar-a-Largo weekends.

That "some island in
the Pacific" is part of
the United States.

Such power I have.
I tweet a name or company
and they rise or fall.

Which is funnier,
Saturday Night Live's Trump
or Trump himself?

92 days in,
473 cabinet appointees short,
explains White House confusion.

Day 92, Trump says
100 day accomplishment lists
are ridiculous.

Campaign promise; I'll
release my tax returns if I win.
He did, he didn't.

Campaign promises;
things you say to be elected
but rarely fulfill.

April 22

Massive tax reform
next week. No particulars given
because there are none.

Palin's in the news
again. As eloquent as
Trump also isn't.

Unlike Truman, the
buck never stops at Trump.
It's not enough.

Another Trump rally
next week to celebrate first
100 days. Has he no shame?

April 24

Will Trump and family
leave the White House richer than
when they entered it?

Trump's tweets are spreading.
Now Sessions joins in with his
fake news and faulty facts.

Logical rarely
applies to anything Trump
says, tweets, does or thinks.

Trump's brain, like a clenched
fist, ready to strike or defend,
never to think.

April 25

Uh-oh. Flynn in news
again; time to drop another
bomb or declare war.

April 26

Trade war with Canada,
maybe real war with North Korea.
All goes well with Trump.

Tax reform plan released.
It won't pass but it looks like
he's doing something.

As Sean Maloney said,
"It's not a tax reform plan,
it's a page!".

Trump's screw the poor, help
the rich get richer tax plan.
Is his base rich?

April 27

Does Trump lie to fool
others or to delude himself?
Does he know he lies?

Trump as misunderstood
Robin Hood, taking from the poor,
giving to the rich.

The primary accomplishment
of Trump's first hundred days;
we, and the world, have survived.

Trump still complaining
about "outrageous courts". If
only he could muzzle them.

April 28

Major tax reform plan;
two hundred words, one page,
no chance in hell to pass.

It's less about what good
Trump has done than what
good he has undone.

Trump will appear before
any applauding crowd. Today
it's the NRA.

It's Obama's fault again,
Trump blaming him for Flynn's
ties to Russia.

April 29

Trump's hundredth day
and of course he says they've been
the most productive in history.

If Trump must be best
at all he does, is being best
worst president good?

If the free press is
our enemy, who are
our friends?

Also by Donald Scheller and Buffalo Arts Publishing:

May, June and All the Years Before, 2012

Portraits & Memories, 2015

Available online at www.buffaloartspublishing.com and www.amazon.com

www.ingramcontent.com/pod-product-compliance
Lightning Source LLC
Chambersburg PA
CBHW052136010526
44113CB00036B/2290